BUFFALO DAYS

BY DIANE HOYT-GOLDSMITH

PHOTOGRAPHS BY LAWRENCE MIGDALE

HOLIDAY HOUSE / NEW YORK

This book is dedicated to the memory of
Rick Sanford of Bridger, Montana
1950 - 1996

Library of Congress Cataloging-in-Publication Data
Hoyt-Goldsmith, Diane.
    Buffalo days / by Diane Hoyt-Goldsmith:
  photographs by Lawrence Migdale.
        p.   cm.
    Summary: Describes life on a Crow Indian reservation in Montana, and the importance these tribes place on buffalo, which are once again thriving in areas where the Crow live.
    ISBN 0-8234-1327-6 (reinforced)
  1. Crow Indians—Juvenile literature
  2. American bison—Juvenile literature
  3. Crow Indian Reservation (Mont.)—Juvenile literature. [1. Crow Indians. 2. Indians of North America—Montana. 3. Bison.] I. Migdale, Lawrence, ill. II. Title.
E99.C92H693   1997   97-13209
978.6'38-dc21   CIP
                                                                           AC

Acknowledgments
We would like to thank our host family, Clarence and Jocelyn Three Irons, and their sons Greg, Cameron, Alvin, Clay, and especially Clarence, Jr. for their help and cooperation in preparing this book.

We appreciate the hospitality and participation of Joe and Charlene Alden, and their children Shannon, Crystal, Leslie, and J.P. We are grateful to Ronald Stewart and Robert Pickett for showing us the fine points of a tipi raising, and we appreciate the participation of Kaylee Three Irons and her mother Kateri, Kyle Whiteman, Shylon Alden, Jessie Old Crow, Jordan White, Brandi Alden, Lauri Kindness, Daphne Alden, and Ruth Backbone. Dancers Kalsey BirdinGround, Marilyn and Marcia Blacksmith, and Gary Plenty Buffalo were wonderful about sharing their beautiful traditional clothing. We appreciate the cooperation of Martin Old Crow and the staff of the Lodge Grass Elementary School.

Thanks also to Joe Medicine Crow for a wonderful interview and his perspectives on the history of the Crow, and to Ben and Marge Pease for reading the manuscript and giving helpful comments. We are grateful to Burton Pretty on Top and Jerome White Hip for their help in documenting the Crow Fair and Rodeo, the Powwow dancers, and the parade.

We would like to thank Fred DuBray of the Wind River Sioux buffalo program for his advice and assistance. Mark Heckert, Director of the InterTribal Bison Cooperative, was good to read our manuscript and give us useful information. To learn more about this organization, contact the InterTribal Bison Cooperative, PO Box 8105, Rapid City, SD 57709, or call 605-394-9730.

We would like to give a special thanks to Charles Westwood, for giving us a bird's eye view from his airplane of the wild buffalo at the top of the Bighorn Mountains. We are also most grateful to Rick Sanford, helicopter pilot, for making it possible to photograph the Crow Fair from the air.

Thanks also to Lorna Mason for her careful reading of the manuscript and suggestions and to Leah Goldsmith for her valuable perpsectives as a "young reader."

Ten-year-old Clarence Three Irons, Jr. rides his pinto horse named Paint almost every day.

Clarence Three Irons, Jr. is a member of the Crow Indian tribe. He lives with his family on a forty-acre ranch near Lodge Grass, Montana. The ranch, where his family raises cattle and horses, is on the Crow Indian Reservation. A hundred and fifty years ago, this land was also the home of huge herds of wild buffalo.

Sometimes Clarence's father uses an ATV, an "all-terrain vehicle," instead of a horse to get around on the ranch. In the valley below is the ranch house where Clarence and his family live.

Like most Crow Indians, Clarence has several names. He was named Clarence after his father when he was born. Later he was given an Indian name by his clan uncle. The Crow believe an Indian name can influence a person's life and future. Clarence's Indian name, Iilappáach Ahóo, means "has many friends." Clarence's clan uncle enjoys the friendship of many people, and by giving Clarence this name, he wishes the same for him.

Clarence also has a nickname that he got from his grandfather. When Clarence's older brothers were in the Head Start program and attending nursery school, they learned to speak English. Clarence, who was just learning to talk, spoke only in the Crow language. His grandfather said he was a real Indian. The name fit and now everyone calls him Indian.

4

Indian lives with his mother, father, and two older brothers, Alvin and Clay. He has two more brothers, Cameron and Greg, who are grown up and live in their own homes nearby. Alvin and Clay are good riders. They enter rodeos to compete in team roping. Indian likes to ride, too. He and his brothers spend a lot of time practicing their rodeo skills in the corral behind their house.

Indian and his brothers Alvin and Clay ride their horses bareback.

Although Indian would much rather be riding his horse than going to school, he tries not to take school for granted. When the Crow reservation was first set up back in 1883, all the Crow Indian children were sent away to a boarding school. At the age of four or five, they would be taken away from their families to live at the school in another town. The Crow people missed their children and protested. Finally in 1903, the government allowed the Crow to set up the nation's first Indian Day School on the reservation. Then the children could go home after school each day to be with their families.

Indian is in the fifth grade at a public school in Lodge Grass, Montana.

◧ BEFORE THE BUFFALO DAYS ◧

The ancestors of the Crow Indians called themselves *Apsáalooke,* which means "Children of the Long-Beaked Bird." When European trappers and explorers first came into contact with the Crow, the only way they could communicate was by sign language. Although the Crow say that the long-beaked bird was really a raven, somehow their name was translated as "Crow" instead. That is why they are called Crow Indians today.

According to Crow legends, their ancestors migrated to this area long ago. Historians believe the migration began in the Eastern woodlands of the United States and lasted for many generations as the Crow wandered from place to place. After about a hundred years, they came to the valley of the Little Bighorn and stayed. Historians agree with Crow oral history in estimating that the Crow have lived in the land of the Bighorn Mountains since the 1700s. To them, it is beautiful country.

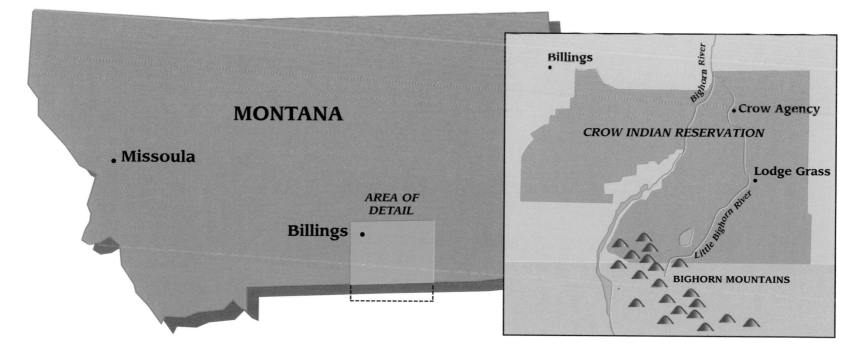

CROW COUNTRY IS IN EXACTLY THE RIGHT PLACE. EVERYTHING GOOD IS TO BE FOUND THERE. THERE IS NO COUNTRY LIKE THE CROW COUNTRY.

Arapooish, Chief of the Crow

The land where the Crow Indians live is lush and fertile. The Bighorn River flows through a valley filled with ranches and farms.

■ THE BUFFALO DAYS ■

When the first horses came to the Crow in about 1730, they dramatically changed the Indians' way of life. According to one legend, a Crow war party traveled as far south as Great Salt Lake and returned with creatures unlike anything the Crow had ever seen before. Horses on the plains were the descendants of those left behind by the Spanish explorer, Coronado. They soon proved to be very useful. Horses helped the Crow to get from place to place quickly and easily. Horses made it possible for the Crow to move their camps, following the buffalo herds as they migrated across the plains.

The Crow became excellent riders and hunters. Buffalo hunters learned to ride at a gallop and shoot a bow and arrow at the same time. Soon the buffalo became the most important animal for the Crow, as well as for the other tribes who lived on the plains.

Joe Medicine Crow was raised by his grandparents, who grew up during the Buffalo Days. Joe's grandparents shared stories with him that made those days come alive. As Joe grew up, he collected his tribe's oral history. He enjoys telling Indian about the past.

9

The buffalo provided many things that the Crow needed. The Crow ate the meat and used the hides to make their tipis, storage containers, and clothing. They wove or braided buffalo hair to make ropes. They shaped the bones into utensils for eating, scrapers, and other tools. The Crow used nearly every part of the buffalo. With the buffalo came a new way of life that the Crow call the Buffalo Days.

When there were plenty of buffalo in Crow country, life was good for the Indians. The buffalo helped the Crow tribe grow strong and prosper.

However, the Buffalo Days did not last. When settlers came to the land of the Crow, they began slaughtering buffalo to make way for their herds of cattle and for the railroads that were being built across the plains. The settlers' new way of life brought fenced ranches for cattle and ownership of land. The free-ranging days of the buffalo on the plains were soon over.

At the time of the first European contact, wild buffalo herds ranged over most of North America. Three hundred years later, the places where buffalo could be found had shrunk considerably. By 1900, the buffalo were nearly extinct in the wild.

Buffalo range in 1500

Buffalo range in 1800

The numbers of buffalo on the prairies was reduced from more than 30 million in 1880 to only a few thousand by 1889. This photograph, taken in about 1895, shows a stack of buffalo skulls at the Michigan Carbon Works in Detroit. Buffalo bones like these were collected on the prairie and shipped to factories where they were ground up for such uses as fertilizer.

In just a little more than a hundred years, 60 million wild buffalo were hunted until they became almost extinct. In Crow country, the last buffalo were killed in 1884. Ten years later, the U.S. Congress finally passed a law that stopped buffalo hunting for good. By then, the only buffalo left were in city zoos, privately owned herds, or national parks.

When the buffalo disappeared, the Crow people, like the Sioux, the Cheyenne, and other Plains tribes, were left without a way to live. With the basis for their livelihood destroyed, the people in these tribes became dependent upon the federal government for food and jobs. It was easy then for the government to force all the Indians to live on reservations. Although the Buffalo Days had not lasted much longer than a hundred years, the Crow would never forget them.

◧ THE BUFFALO RETURN ◧

Today wild buffalo herds are coming back to the Indian reservations. Native Americans from many different tribes all over the United States and Canada are helping the herds grow. They believe that the return of the buffalo will bring prosperity, as well as a new sense of pride, to Indian people. Like the buffalo, the Crow and other Plains Indians are survivors.

The Crow tribe's wild herd started in the 1930s when they arranged to bring in several hundred animals to start a herd. Some of the buffalo came from Yellowstone Park, some from the National Bison Range in Montana, and a few from private individuals.

Today, Indian's father works for the Crow tribe as a buffalo manager. He helps to take care of the wild herd that lives at the top of the Bighorn Mountains on the reservation. It is not an easy job. Buffalo are hard to control. They are so big and strong that they can run right through the kind of fence that would hold a herd of cattle.

Luckily, the Crow have a place on their reservation that is perfect for a buffalo pasture. High on the top of the Bighorn Mountains, west of Lodge Grass, there are thirty thousand acres of wilderness. The pasture is twelve miles wide, and it is surrounded on three sides by deep canyons. Along the fourth side, the tribe has built a giant, ten-foot-high steel fence.

Weighing as much as two thousand pounds each, buffalo need a large area for grazing. The deep canyons surrounding the buffalo pasture keep the herd from wandering away.

Indian and his father travel on ATVs to patrol the many acres of pastureland where the buffalo live, wild and free, isolated from the cattle ranches in the valleys below.

One problem that the buffalo managers must deal with is disease. When settlers brought cattle to the plains in the late 1800s, some of the cattle diseases spread to wild animals. One of these, called brucellosis, can infect buffalo as well as elk and deer. To solve problems like these, the Crow Nation joined an organization that is called the InterTribal Bison Cooperative.

14

This is a group of more than forty Indian tribes that is working together to find ways to bring the buffalo back to their reservations and make them a part of Indian life once again. Today, members of the cooperative are managing more than ten thousand buffalo on reservations all over the United States.

The cooperative has developed many different plans to keep their herds healthy. One of these is a buffalo roundup. Each autumn, tribes all over the country herd the wild buffalo into huge pens. The new calves are examined and vaccinated against brucellosis and other diseases.

On a visit to the buffalo pasture, Indian's father tells him about the ancient Crow buffalo jumps. Long ago, before they had horses to chase after buffalo, the Crow worked together to herd animals over a cliff. Then they butchered the ones that fell to their deaths below. There are other old buffalo jumps on the Crow reservation.

■ THE BUFFALO ROUNDUP ■

The buffalo roundup takes place at the end of the summer each year. Before winter snows make the roads impassable, members of the Crow tribe travel up into the mountains to the buffalo pasture. Indian's father lets him come along to help.

For the roundup, the Crow people use modern technology. The tribe uses a helicopter to spot small herds hiding in the ravines and forests. Some people drive all-terrain vehicles in the roundup, while others, like Indian and his father, ride on horseback.

The loud, unfamiliar noise of a helicopter makes the buffalo start to run. Then teams of cowboys track and herd the buffalo toward the holding pens.

Members of the Crow tribe herd the wild buffalo into the holding pens they have built at the buffalo pasture. It takes several days to round up all the buffalo. At night, the cowboys sleep in a bunkhouse or in tipis set up near the corrals.

(Below) Indian's father uses a cellular phone to communicate between the buffalo pasture and his office in Crow Agency.

(Left) Indian helps out during the roundup by carrying messages and supplies from one part of the corral to another.

Once inside the holding pens, the animals are examined and vaccinated. All the buffalo are counted and a record is kept of the number of males and females. The Crow herd has grown from nine hundred in 1990 to twelve hundred in 1995.

A great deal of good has come from the return of the buffalo to Crow country. First of all, their sharp hooves break up the soil in the buffalo pasture, providing places where seeds can fall and start to grow. Buffalo dung is a natural fertilizer. These big animals graze so that the tallest prairie grasses are left untouched. Indian's father says that buffalo habits are good for the earth.

Buffalo meat is an important food source for the Crow, especially on important ceremonial occasions, such as the Sun Dance that is held in the summer. Buffalo skulls are kept for use in their ceremonies as well. Sometimes the Crow sell buffalo meat to supermarkets outside the reservation. Buffalo meat is becoming more popular because it has less fat and more protein than beef, and less cholesterol than chicken.

Indian's father ropes a young buffalo calf. Then other members of the tribe give it a vaccination.

Sometimes young buffalo bulls or cows are sold to tribes in other parts of the country. The money from these sales helps to finance the care of the Crow herd and to buy things that the tribe needs. One year, the tribe used the buffalo money to buy a few pickup trucks.

Best of all, the buffalo are a link to the past. They remind Indian and his tribe of the Buffalo Days, a time when life was good for the Crow people.

CELEBRATING ⬛ THE BUFFALO DAYS ⬛

Every summer the Crow nation holds a special gathering to celebrate the Buffalo Days. The Crow Fair and Rodeo is something that Indian's whole family looks forward to all year long. The fair began in 1904 as a way to encourage ranching and farming. Over the years, it has become a celebration of Native American traditions. People who come to the fair are able to experience a way of life that existed during the Buffalo Days.

During the third week in August, Crow people from all over the reservation gather to put up their tipis. They hold a powwow that lasts for many days, with dance contests, drumming, and giveaways. There are rodeo competitions and horse races every day. People from other tribes all over North America come to share in the fun.

(Right) The Crow Fair and Rodeo is called the Tipi Capital of the World as people put up more than a thousand tipis on the fairgrounds.

These girls perform in a Fancy Shawl Dance.

■ SETTING UP A TIPI ■

Setting up a tipi is a hard job that takes three or four people working together.

During the Buffalo Days, tipis were made from tanned buffalo hides. Today, tipis are made from white canvas fabric. The tall, slender trunks of lodgepole pine trees provide the tipi frame. For each tipi, Indian's family needs twenty-three poles, each one at least twenty-seven feet long.

Indian enjoys sleeping inside a tipi. He can look up at the night sky and see the stars through the vent hole at the top. During the day, the sun shines through the canvas and makes the tipi glow like a lamp. A tipi gives him privacy, but Indian can also hear what is going on outside. He listens to the birds singing in the twilight or the soft voices of people talking around the campfire. In the morning, he wakes up to the sun.

For the Crow people, a tipi is more than just a shelter. It is a symbol of a way of life now gone from their everyday world. Staying in a tipi gives them a chance to appreciate and understand the culture of their ancestors.

First, the family ties together the four main poles. These poles are stronger than all the others.

Next, Indian watches as the poles are pushed into an upright position.

Then, one by one, Indian helps his father add the long tipi poles to the frame.

Finally, they unfold the canvas tipi cover and wrap it around the frame. The door of the tipi always faces east, where the sun rises in the morning.

One of Indian's jobs is to use handmade stakes to anchor the cover to the ground.

Staying in their tipis in the encampment, the kids learn what it is like to live close to their relatives and friends. For a brief time each summer, they stay up as late as they like. When they finally fall asleep, it is to the sounds of drumming and dancing.

Indian and his brother Greg pay a visit to their grandmother in her tipi. A buffalo robe on the floor makes her lodge a cozy place to sit.

Indian's family brings horses with them to camp. Indian spends much of the day riding with his cousin J.P.

Indian and his friends eat Indian tacos, a meal made by putting spicy beans, chopped lettuce and tomatoes, and salsa on a piece of fry bread.

Each morning, there is a parade around the tipi camp. Dressed in their finest traditional clothing, the Crow ride around the camp on their horses. It is a time for everyone, young and old, to show pride in their heritage.

Indian's brother Cameron helps him get ready for the parade.

Indian's mother cleans a deerskin garment by scraping the surface with a knife.

Indian and members of his family wait for the parade around the camp to begin.

After the parade, awards are given for the best outfits in various categories. Indian's niece, Kaylee, won twenty-five dollars for the best-dressed rider under the age of twelve. She is only eight months old, but like many Crow children, she is already getting used to riding a horse. She has a special saddle with a safety belt attached.

27

(Top Left) Gary Plenty Buffalo from Lodge Grass wears a Grass Dance outfit. His headdress is made of porcupine hair and he wears eagle feathers. When he dances, the fringe on his apron and leggings move like grass in the wind.

(Top Right) Kalsey BirdinGround from Crow Agency wears a Jingle Dance dress. The jingles on her dress are made from the tops of tin cans that have been shaped into cones.

(Bottom Left) Marcia Blacksmith from Lodge Grass wears a traditional Crow dress decorated with elk teeth. She holds a fan of hawk feathers and a hand-bag decorated with bead-work.

(Bottom Right) Marilyn Blacksmith is Marcia's older sister. She wears an outfit for the Fancy Shawl Dance. There are mink tails braided into her hair, and she wears a white eagle feather.

Each day during the Crow Fair, hundreds of Native American dancers from all over the West compete in different categories. People of all ages come to perform and to watch. For everyone, it is a time to celebrate the best of their traditions and to keep those traditions alive.

Indian wears traditional clothing including a special headdress called a roach. This is made from porcupine hair. His brightly colored arm-bands are decorated with handmade, beaded designs. Because Indian has short hair, he wears a braided wig when he dresses as his ancestors once did.

Indian loves it at the Crow Fair. Living in a tipi and wearing traditional clothing puts him in touch with the lifeways of his ancestors. His parents, and the generations that came before them, have worked hard to preserve Crow traditions. For this, Indian is very thankful. He is also happy that the Crow have a wild buffalo herd living at the top of the Bighorn Mountains. They are another link to the past and a reminder that it is good to live in the land of the Crow.

GLOSSARY

Apsáalooke (Ap-SAH-lah-gah) The Crow name for themselves. It means "Children of the Long-Beaked Bird."

ATV Short for "all-terrain vehicle," a versatile four-wheel-drive vehicle used to travel in places where the roads are very rough or nonexistent.

bison (BY-sen) Another term for buffalo.

boarding school A school away from home at which the students live.

brucellosis (broo-cel-OH-sis) A contagious disease in cattle that also affects wild animals such as buffalo and elk.

buffalo A four-legged animal with a shaggy mane and a humped back, once common in North America but hunted to near extinction in the late 1800s.

buffalo jump A natural feature in the landscape, such as a cliff, where American Indians stampeded buffalo, making them jump to their deaths. The animals were then used for their meat, bones, and hides.

canyon A long, narrow valley between two high cliffs.

Cheyenne (shy-AN) A tribe of Plains Indians, many of whom live in Montana.

Crow (CROH) A tribe of Plains Indians, many of whom live on a reservation in southeastern Montana.

Iilappáach Ahóo (EE-lah-PAH-jah ah-HOH) The name given to Clarence Three Irons, Jr. It means "has many friends" in the Crow language.

InterTribal Bison Cooperative An organization founded in 1991 with more than forty Native American tribes as members. The tribes work together to bring buffalo herds back to their reservations.

oral history Legends and stories about people and past events that are passed from generation to generation by spoken language.

pinto A descriptive term for a horse that is white with black or brown patches.

reservation Public land set aside by the federal government as a place for American Indian people to live.

roach A special headdress worn by Crow Indian men and boys, usually made from porcupine hairs.

Sioux (SOO) A tribe of Plains Indians, many of whom live in Montana, North and South Dakota.

tipi (TEE-pee) A cone-shaped tent dwelling once made from buffalo hides and used by the Plains Indian tribes. Today tipis are made of canvas cloth.

vaccination An injection of a drug or vaccine using a syringe and needle to give immunity against a disease.

INDEX

Page numbers in italic type refer to photographs.

THE BUFFALO MEANS EVERYTHING TO THE CROW. NOT ONLY DO WE NOW HAVE MEAT FOR OUR CELEBRATIONS, BUT WE EAT THE MEAT AND IT MAKES US FEEL GOOD. WE TAN THE HIDES. WE KEEP THE SKULLS. IT JUST MAKES US FEEL INDIAN AGAIN. WE LOST A PART OF OUR WAY OF LIFE, OUR CULTURE. NOW IT MAKES EVEN LITTLE KIDS HAPPY TO KNOW WE HAVE BUFFALO RUNNING UP THERE.

JOE MEDICINE CROW